Painter's Pocket Reference
Trees

Essential tips and techniques for rendering better trees

Patricia Seligman

APPLE

A QUARTO BOOK

Copyright © 1997
Quarto Publishing plc

Published by The Apple Press
6 Blundell Street
London N7 9BH

This book was designed and produced by
Quarto Publishing plc
The Old Brewery
6 Blundell Street
London N7 9BH

ISBN 1-85076-932-X

First printed 1997

Printed in China by
Leefung Asco Printers Ltd.

CONTENTS

UNDERSTANDING THE BASICS

4   Simplifying trees

6   Light

7   Perspective

8   Color

SEASONAL DIRECTORY

12 **A WINTER SCENE**

14 Maple

18 Oak

22 Beech

26 **ASPEN**

32 Apple tree

TREE DIRECTORY	

36	**BROAD-LEAF TREES**	49	Redwood
38	Ash	50	Fir
39	Elm	51	Cedar
40	Poplar	**52**	**PALMS**
41	Sycamore plane	54	Date
42	Willow	55	Coconut
43	Eucalyptus gum tree	56	Fan
44	Horse chestnut	57	Solid-leaf banana
45	Olive	**58**	**FLOWER AND FRUIT TREES**
46	**CONIFERS**	60	Orange
48	Cypress	61	Magnolia
		62	Fig
		63	Cherry
		64	Credits

UNDERSTANDING THE BASICS

When painting, an artist not only has to simplify the image he or she sees, but also to choose and mix the colors to represent reality. This process involves many decisions not only for the beginner but also for the professional artist of many years' experience. Knowledge of the subject helps with these decisions and in this section we look at the process of simplification—or "characterization"—of trees: their shapes, trunks, branches, leaves. We also examine the effects of light on trees, perspective and the use of color.

SIMPLIFYING TREES

When an artist paints a tree, he or she will be providing a number of pieces of information which, when pieced together, will make it possible for the viewer to tell the exact species of tree. It is not just the shape of a tree that gives a clue to its species, but also its height, spread, foliage, color, not to mention details such as the density of the canopy, the texture of the bark and variations in the buds, flowers, fruit and seeds. A tree in the distance will often be summarily expressed with a few brushstrokes and an absence of detail, but with the knowledge of the main characteristics of a tree the artist can still hint at a great deal.

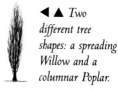

◀ ▲ *Two different tree shapes: a spreading Willow and a columnar Poplar.*

▲ *A blighted ash showing the pattern of branches.*

Shape

Let us first look at the shape of trees. Trees fall into various categories of shapes but they can also be a combination of two, such as the Californian redwood which is both columnar and conic. Bear these shapes in mind when sketching trees.

Trunk and branches

Notice the variation of trunk and branches in different trees. Some start and divide low down the trunk, as in the oak; others begin higher up so a great deal of the trunk is visible, as in the eucalyptus. The pattern of the branches differs, too, with some growing from a point in the trunk of the tree and then fanning out, as they do in the maple, while the branches of the American sycamore spring from the central trunk roughly parallel to the ground. Some branches taper quickly with upturned tips, others arch and have drooping tips. The branches of the English oak grow in craggy fits and starts, while the branches of other trees sprout in smooth transition from branch to twig.

Canopy and leaves

The outline and density of the canopy is very telling. The outline is sometimes clear and solid like that of the maple, or rather rugged and unsure of itself, like that of the eucalyptus. Leaves also differ enormously in size, color and their powers of reflection. Some trees have dull leaves which absorb the light, while others have a shiny surface which catches the light, making the tree look as if it is sparkling after a rainstorm.

Catching these differences in paint often means simplifying the foliage through textural techniques, such as, sponging, stippling or drybrush (see the Directory).

▲ *Whorls and scars relate the history of the tree.*

▲ *Palm trees have a distinctive canopy.*

▶ *The oak leaf is lost in the canopy.*

Bark

Study the bark of trees; there is an amazing variation in color and texture, from the smooth, dappled appearance of the trunk of the plane tree like watercolor washes, to the deep, furrowed ridges of the oak, more like dark, impasto acrylic relief. In winter, such detail can be important in the foreground of a picture, but most of the time you will be giving an impression of a tree from a distance. Even then, though, the color and the ability of the bark to reflect light can give you clues as to the species of tree. There are suggestions for color mixes for tree bark on page 11.

LIGHT

Light gives three-dimensional objects their form. When painting a tree, first work out the direction of the cast light so that you can place the highlights on the surface of the tree closest to the light source and the shadows on the other side. With opaque paints, you can work from the darker parts of the tree, adding the brightest highlights right at the end. With watercolors, you usually work from the palest parts, building up washes to create the darkest shadows. In bright light, contrasts in tone will be more pronounced. In dull lights, the range of contrasts will be narrower but a greater variation of subtle mid-tones will be visible. Notice, too, how light not only varies in strength but also in color.

▲ ▶ *The direction and strength of the light affects the composition.*

PERSPECTIVE

The principles of linear perspective are always useful when plotting a line of trees receding down an avenue into the distance, or a felled tree on the ground, or when depicting a tree viewed from beneath, looking up its trunk. In its simplest form, linear perspective states that where parallel lines are seen traveling away from a fixed point, they appear to converge at a point on the horizon. Following such rules can help you to work out—or at least check —the artist's more usual way of creating prespective through observation. Certainly, if a branch is coming out towards you from the trunk of a tree, observation is your only hope. Take heart that the most carefully formulated drawings often don't look right and need to be tinkered with to make them "work."

Aerial and atmospheric perspective

Perhaps more useful to the painter of trees and

Background

Middle ground

Foreground

▲ *Simplify your approach and divide up your view into three parts.*

▼ *Unusual perspectives make interesting compositions.*

landscapes are those guiding rules controlling the creation of an illusion of recession in the picture space. Based again on observation, these rules state that over distance detail diminishes, contours lose their definition, colors become less saturated (weaker), cooler and bluer, and that contrasts are reduced.

It often helps to simplify your view by dividing it into foreground, middle ground and distance, treating each of these parts as steps into the picture space—rather like receding scenery on a stage. In the foreground, trees will be easier to identify as individual species. Colors will be brighter and warmer and contrasts wider in tone. In the middle ground, trees will be less detailed and seen as groups, colors will be less saturated and cooler and contrasts narrower. Distant trees will be generalized as forests and woods, colors will be even cooler and paler and contrasts even narrower.

COLOR

One glance at the Directory will remind you that trees come not only in many different shapes but also in an unexpected range of colors. It is easy to fall into the trap of painting trees a mid-green, ignoring the information presented to you in the tree itself. The artist has to keep an open mind and record what he or she sees, rather than expects to see. In the course of a single day, under the effect of the prevailing light on color, a mid-green tree can appear to pass through all the colors of the rainbow. Even in a clear mid-strength light, trees vary in the green of their foliage.

▲ *Paul Kenny, Summer Wood, gouache. Pinks, ocher, browns and greens combine in this bank of foliage.*

▼ *David Carr, Chestnut, gouache. The red underpainting shows through in places complementing the rich blue greens.*

▼ *R. Jestey, Slepe Copse, watercolor. Yellow greens of a hot summer's day.*

Foliage colors

Artists find that if greens for painting trees are mixed rather than taken straight from a ready-mixed tube or pan, more vibrant greens will result, if only because elements of the constituent colors will make them more interesting. Consequently, the precise green is often mixed on the canvas, optically, by superimposing thin washes of watercolor, by stippling acrylic colors together or by scumbling one pastel color over another.

Interesting foliage colors can be created by building up over an underpainting laid down in complementary colors—red for the foliage, with greens worked over the top.

In the Directory, the palette of each artist is described and gives an idea of how many different ways there are to create greens.

▲ *Super-imposed wash*

▲ *Pastel scumbling*

▲ *Stipple with acrylic paints*

▲ *Glazing oil paints*

"Tube" greens

It is also worth investigating available tube or pan greens which can save you a lot of time, to be dulled with complementary red or lightened with a touch of yellow.

Two useful greens found in all media are sap and viridian green. It is surprising how these colors can vary between the different media and manufacturers in appearance and in their behavior. Sap green is a good mid-green, wonderfully transparent in oil and therefore good for glazing, but less transparent in acrylic. It mixes well, i.e. it retains its strength and vibrancy. Viridian (or Phthalocyanine green), a strong blue-green, is also transparent in its oil version. It is a dominating color, however, and has to be used with care.

Other greens worth investigating are terre verte, a dull, earth green (not gouache or acrylic), olive green, a dark, earthy brown-green (not oil or acrylic) and oxide of chromium, a dull, opaque blue-green (not acrylic).

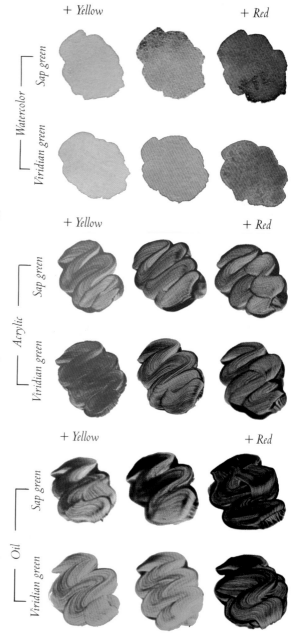

+ Yellow   *+ Red*

Watercolor — *Sap green* / *Viridian green*

+ Yellow   *+ Red*

Acrylic — *Sap green* / *Viridian green*

+ Yellow   *+ Red*

Oil — *Sap green* / *Viridian green*

Bark mixes

The strength and color of the prevailing light will greatly effect the "color" of a tree's trunk and branches. Look at the examples in the Directory to see how different they appear and how each artist interprets those variations. Bark is rarely just plain, flat brown. A trunk is rounded and often scarred and irregular so that the play of light gives variations in the color. Bark is often green, silver or red, or encrusted with ocher lichens. The color is further affected by the bark's texture, be it smooth, ridged, furrowed or peeling.

Be creative with your mixes. Try indigo, alizarin crimson and yellow ocher for dark mixes of red-brown. In the distance, the same species of tree will appear paler and bluer so perhaps ultramarine with a touch of yellow ocher will be appropriate. Viridian and burnt sienna, on the other hand, produce a good color or, for a more powerful electric performance, try the complementaries, violet and pale lemon yellow.

SEASONAL DIRECTORY

In this section we look at a selection of trees which have been painted through the seasons, in spring, summer, fall and winter. This will enable you to see how a tree changes through the seasons—the color and density of the canopy varies widely which affects the proportions of the bare wood as seen in winter.

A WINTER SCENE

The shape of the winter trees varies enormously from species to species. It is worth studying the precise shape of an individual tree as this will give your work variety. In this painting, notice how effectively the pale hues of the sky "shine" through the negative shapes between the branches.

▼ *Bart O'Farell, Snow, St. Keverne, acrylic.*

▼ *The pale winter sky contrasts dramatically with the dark silhouette of intricate branches, giving depth to the painting. Delicate flecks of pale gray cloud have been painted over the light blues and yellow to create a mid-tone, which balances the composition.*

▲ *The main branches gradually taper into finer twigs to form the tree canopy. Once the artist established these solid verticals, which form the main structure of the trees, he was able to start building up the delicate network of smaller branches using a very fine bristle brush.*

▶ *Striking tonal contrasts have been used to great effect. Notice how the darkest darks of the tree trunks are juxtaposed with the lightest lights of the sky and pale sepia grass, drawing your eye towards the center of the picture.*

13

EARLY TINGES OF COLOR

The Norway maple, common in Europe and similar to the American sugar maple, flowers in April before the leaves appear, giving the branches a yellowish tinge. The young leaves are pale green at first, darkening as they fill out. Lay down the pale yellow color first and work in hints of the darker branches, suggesting the shape of the tree rather than individual twigs. Using opaque gouache, sky holes can be added showing through the sparser spring canopy.

Linden green

Burnt umber

Oxide of chromium

Skyholes— gouache

1 *The yellow spring foliage and dark colors of the background wood are built up wet-in-wet.*

2 *As the spring canopy is sparse, more sky holes are added over the dry foliage in cobalt blue.*

3 *Notice how touches of white paper show through over the whole picture surface enlivening the painting.*

BREAKING UP THE CANOPY

In full summer, the sugar maple's rich green canopy almost hides the branches. Glimpses of the branches and small patches of the sky—"sky holes"—can be seen between the leaves, and note how the trunk appears shorter as the canopy comes down to cover it. In most species of maple, the shape of the canopy is more cylindrical than spreading. You cannot add every detail of every leaf on a tree but by building up a general background of the canopy color you can then add suggestions of leaf details at the end.

Brilliant yellow green

Sap green

Naples yellow

Simplifying detail—acrylic

1 *First build up the dark background in soft dry layers of deep violet, phthalo blue and burnt sienna.*

2 *When dry, superimpose greens and add branches, reinforcing the shape of the dark trunk with pale green either side.*

3 *Finally, add touches of palest green with a small brush to indicate details of the leaf canopy.*

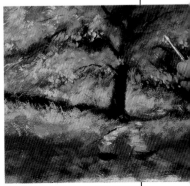

15

FALL DISPLAY

Attracting visitors from far away, the show of color produced by the North American maple in the fall is well known, inspiring artists to paint it. Here the artist varies the color mix and the dilution as the fiery canopy evolves rather than superimposing layers. Artists often have personalized techniques and tools. Here an old customized wooden spoon is used to draw out the paint for those branches and twigs which involved abrupt twists and turns. Any hard, blunt-ended instrument will do.

Sepia

Prussian blue

Burnt umber

Olive green

MAPLE

Leaf shapes—watercolor

1 *Characterize the maple leaves with three touches of a round brush, varying the dilution of the paint.*

2 *For the trunk raw umber, Prussian blue and sepia are loosely applied with a brush and then drawn out with a wooden "spoon."*

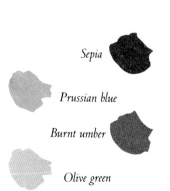

3 *The leaf shape is enforced with a dip pen loaded with watercolor.*

WINTER BRANCHES

The branches of the maple are not very heavy and grow low down out of the main trunk. The twigs develop straighter and finer compared with those of the oak. The bark of the sugar maple is pale gray, and is rough with furrows, and scaly ridges whereas the Norway maple is browner and more finely ridged. When painting a bare winter tree in watercolor, work in the main trunk and branches with a fine brush, and then use a dip pen filled with watercolor for the fine tracery of the end twigs.

Ultramarine blue

Indian yellow

Burnt sienna

Raw sienna

Dip pen—watercolor

1 *Over the dry background washes, paint the main branches of the young maple.*

2 *Using a brush, fill a steel-nibbed dip pen with watercolor. Try it out first and then map out the thinner branches.*

3 *Notice how the darker tones have been built up around the highlights, as around the trunk of the tree.*

17

SPRING COLORS

When spring bursts forth, the stark winter branches of the English oak will appear to soften as the buds open and the young leaves unfurl. These are often brightly colored— even a deep red—and male catkins dangling from twig tips add a yellow tinge to the form. The first hint of spring is revealed in the quality of light, which affects the color mixes. You can convey the early signs of spring by painting with a dry brush over the general winter shape of the oak, softening the outline with hints of red, yellow and green.

Stippling— acrylic

1 *With a flat brush, paint in the structure of the tree—the trunk and larger branches which grow in angular spurts.*

2 *Gradually build up the tree, using smaller brushes for smaller branches and finally, for the twigs, a graphite pencil.*

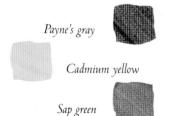

3 *To add the bloom of the early leaf growth, use a long flat brush and a yellow-green, stippling on the leaves in different sizes.*

Payne's gray

Cadmium yellow

Sap green

SUMMER CANOPY

The stout trunk of the oak almost disappears under the thick, lush summer canopy, and there are only glimpses of the branches. Summer leaves are very different in color between species as can be seen in a mixed deciduous wood. The leaves of the English oak are a dark green, leaning towards blue. If you add zinc white to watercolor you will have a gouache equivalent. Here the canopy of the oak is built up in gouache over a watercolor sky, from a mid-tone to dark, and then from a paler mid-tone to light. Each successive layer is added once the previous layer is dry, wet on dry.

Prussian blue

Sap green

Raw umber

Wet-on-dry—gouache

1 *Feather on the first two layers, one light, the next darker, using the same mix. Keep the outline broken.*

2 *Add the trunk, then repeat Step 1 with a bright yellow-green, adding the final layer with the tip of the brush in tiny dots.*

3 *By building up wet-on-dry, a sense of three dimensions emerges. The final layer creates the points of light visible in the moving tree.*

19

FALL COLOR

In the fall, the leaves of the English oak turn yellow and then brown, falling late, in great profusion. Other species such as the North American scarlet oak and the red oak, are renowned for their dramatic autumnal color. From a distance, the acorns are not visible on the tree, but give the fallen leaves beneath it a certain texture. With oil paints, leaf colors, best when just turning, can be added wet-in-wet to build up a fresh gradation of color with the brushmarks still intact.

Raw sienna

Oxide of chromium

Cadmium yellow deep hue

Raw umber

OAK

Wet-in-wet—oil

1 *With lively brushwork, loosely establish the masses of foliage and the main structure of the tree.*

2 *Work up the color with gradually thicker paint, wet-in-wet, keeping aware of the shape of the tree.*

3 *The darks in the trunk and visible branches are re-established, tying together the expressive brush work.*

BARE WINTER TREE

The trunk of the English oak is short and stout with heavy widespreading branches and a broad, domed, open crown. The dark, gray-brown bark is rough and has deep, irregular ridges, sometimes superimposed by a layer of dry green lichen. The shape of the winter tree varies enormously from species to species. It is worth taking trouble with the precise shape of an individual tree as this will give your work variety, distinguishing it from more predictable tree shapes that are reproduced by formula.

Ultramarine blue

New gamboge

Sepia

Masking—watercolor

1 *The main bole of the oak has been sketched and masking fluid reserves areas of white snow.*

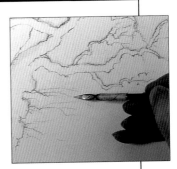

2 *A sky wash is allowed to dry and then the violets and browns of the trunk are added wet-in-wet.*

3 *Remove the masking fluid with a tissue or putty rubber, and then match the snowy highlights with equally dark areas of shadow.*

SPRING CATKINS

A large tree, the American beech grows to 100ft (30m). It has a rounded crown with compact branches, which appear yellow in spring due to the catkins and early, pale green leaves. When using pastels, colors are best mixed optically on the support (the surface on which you are drawing). Small strokes of color can be dotted over the winter shape of the tree to indicate the catkins and new leaves.

Olive green

Indigo

Lemon yellow

Hooker's green

Points of color—pastel

1 *Establish the darker tones of the beech seen contre-jour on the gray tinted pastel paper.*

2 *Now add points of pale yellow light to show through the sparse spring foliage. Turn the pastel stick as you lift it off.*

3 *The pale evening light pervades the painting, touching all elements of the landscape and reflecting in the water.*

COPPER TINTS

With both the American and European beech, the canopy is a regular shape, dense with horizontal breaks. The leaves are toothed and rich green in color. Leaves tend to grow darker and less lush—and therefore reflective—as the summer progresses, particularly in a polluted city. The copper beech, a variety of the European, is a deep purple red in full summer but, depending on the quality of the light, it changes from almost black to red-green. Thin glazes of superimposed acrylic paint can build up the depth of color required.

Cadmium red deep

Raw umber

Raw sienna

Sap green

Glazed washes— acrylics

1 *Apply a thin uneven layer of mid-tone copper brown. Use the more transparent hues and do not add white.*

2 *When the previous layer is dry, add more and increasingly darker transparent glazes, building up a richness of color.*

3 *With final dark glazes added, re-establish the important outline of the tree by cutting in with the sky color. Touch in sky holes with a pointed brush.*

23

Fall Color and Beechnuts

The fall color of the American beech is yellow, while the European beech has reddish brown leaves which sometimes stay on the branches until the new leaves form, rustling dryly in the winter winds. Beechnuts, cased in prickly burrs, ripen in the fall, attracting squirrels. With watercolor, a flat effect can be avoided by adding one color into another wet-in-wet and then superimpose wet-on-dry. Experiment with how long you leave the first layer before you add the second and so on.

New gamboge

Indian red

Ultramarine blue

Burnt umber

Building up washes— watercolor

1 *With a large, soft brush, lay in background washes, feeding one color into another wet-in-wet.*

2 *Once dry, use a 1in (2.5cm) decorator's brush to add mid-tone foliage, allowing the first wash to show through.*

3 *Again allow to dry and add darks. Then, with a fine-pointed sable held vertically, add details of branches.*

24

SNOW-COVERED BRANCHES

Beech trees are easy to distinguish from other large hardwood trees by their smooth bark, which is pale gray and thin. The branches of the European beech come from a solid trunk, spreading out densely in a fan-like way with slender twigs which appear to interlace at the ends of the branches. The American beech is wider-spreading and not quite so dense. Simplify the complicated tracery of twigs with sketchy strokes made with the side of a flat brush.

Cerulean blue

Yellow ocher

Olive green

Payne's gray

Simplifying twigs— watercolor

1 *Paint in the trunk and branches drawing out the twigs with a finger nail. Vary the mix and blot it randomly with a tissue to indicate the play of light.*

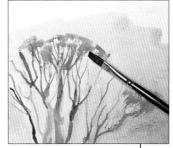

2 *For the intricate tracery of twigs at the end, use a flat brush sideways pulling it over the paper towards the trunk.*

3 *Over darker patches of background, re-establish lost highlights with a white pastel chalk.*

ASPEN

Found all over North America and in Scotland, the quaking aspen, from the poplar family, gets its name from the sensitivity of the leaves which dance to the slightest breeze. This movement is emphasized by the pale underside of the leaves, which are more visible when disturbed.

▲ *Martha Saudek, A day in early spring, oil.*

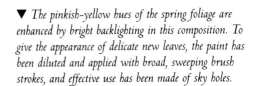

▼ *The pinkish-yellow hues of the spring foliage are enhanced by bright backlighting in this composition. To give the appearance of delicate new leaves, the paint has been diluted and applied with broad, sweeping brush strokes, and effective use has been made of sky holes.*

▲ *The texture of these mottled silver-gray tree trunks was achieved by applying the darker tones first, then adding lighter shades with rough brush strokes once the paint had dried. The brilliant white of the sky peeping through the trunks is the lightest tone of all.*

◀ *The cool purple of the distant trees throws the bright green bush forward, creating a pleasing sense of perspective. This fresh green foliage was a mixture of cadmium yellow lemon and a little sap green.*

SPRING UNFURLING

For the aspen, spring is heralded with pendulous catkins at the tips of most shoots, and the unfurling of leaves which are red-brown to start with. This hint of color on the bare tree can be delicately suggested with pastels in broken color, keeping the pastel strokes clean, without blending or smudging.

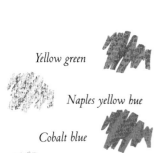

Yellow green

Naples yellow hue

Cobalt blue

White

Broken color— pastel

1 *Build up the background wood and base color of the aspen in broken color without blending.*

2 *Touches of yellow green foliage are added into the base color.*

3 *To keep the focus on the trees, the bluebell glade is blended in places to produce a softer image.*

QUAKING ASPEN

The gray-green leaf is small so that the canopy is light and broken around the edge, barely covering the branches. Movement is relatively easy to portray as the wind bends the aspen's slender trunk and branches, and the canopy is lit up with points of light from the silver-green undersides of the leaves. Stippling on the texture of the leaves in shades of green will give the impression of this light canopy.

Leaf texture—watercolor

1 Describe the fluttering aspen canopy with a stippled mark then work into it with a palette knife for added texture.

2 Add the trunks and hints of the branches, blotting them with a tissue to indicate the silver bark.

3 Working the background around the canopy allows you to redefine the edge. Balance the highlights with small stippled touches of dark shadow.

New gamboge

Payne's gray

Sap green

Olive green

GOLDEN LIGHTS

The quaking aspen is also known as the golden aspen, a name which becomes self-explanatory in the fall when the leaves turn a breathtaking yellow so that the tree looks alive with golden lights. Try using pastels on coarse paper, and scumble lighter colors over murky browns. To preserve the purity of the superimposed yellows, fix the under-layer. With acrylics, try sponging on the foliage color with a natural sponge. You will have to practice first to get the right consistency of the paint and the right pressure on the sponge.

Cadmium yellow

Cerulean blue

Naples yellow

Phthalocyanine green

Sponging—acrylic

1 *Lay on flat background colors. Keep them dark as a contrast to the golden aspen foliage to be superimposed.*

2 *Lay in the silver aspen trunk and then start sponging on the foliage with a small natural sponge.*

3 *Build up the sponging from dark to light. Vary the mark by changing the angle of, and pressure on, the sponge.*

EXPRESSIVE WINTER FORM

In the cold misty light, the further trees are less visible with softer outlines. A useful trick is used here by working wet-in-wet in the distance and wet-on-dry in the foreground. This is easier to manage on a hot day when the initial wash is drying as you proceed and you don't need to wait for it.

Edges— watercolor

1 *Over a wash, add the aspen shapes, wet-in-wet in the distance, wet-on-dry in the foreground.*

2 *Again, with the paint drying, add the trunks and branches with a fine, pointed sable brush, starting in the distance.*

3 *Once dry, with a dry brush build up the soft crowns of the trees then cut in the hedge around the trunks.*

Prussian blue

New gamboge

Crimson red

Payne's gray

31

BLOSSOM TIME

Apple blossom is not as dense as that of cherry or some of the prunuses, so that the tree will appear to be sprinkled with sugar rather than clothed in a dense layer of frosting. In early spring, the pink-tinged blossom predominates until the gray-green leaves take over. Pastels are a natural choice for an apple tree in bloom. Lay down darker color, blending to a flat layer, then stipple over the blossom in pale creams and pinks. Take care not to overdo the contrasts—the "white" blossom will be far from pure white.

Stippling—pastel

1 *On pale gray pastel paper, feel for the structure of the tree and set it in background mid-tones.*

2 *Build up the background foliage, working from dark to light. Add final blue-white blossom with abrupt, stippling strokes.*

3 *As this small sketch proceeded, the colors became more saturated because of increased pressure, and the strokes became smaller and sharper.*

Sepia

Vandyke brown

White

SUMMER ORCHARD

Apple trees do not grow very big and are pruned to keep the fruit within reach. The essence of summer is encapsulated in the rich green canopy of the apple tree, dotted with the growing fruit. You can spatter dilute color into a flatter area of color to create texture or relief which would suit this subject.

Cadmium yellow

Winsor purple

Olive green

Sepia

Burnt umber

Spatter— watercolor

1 Having established early soft background washes, add hints of detail to inform the eye.

2 Mix a dark wash and, with a decorator's brush, run your finger along the bristles to spatter the paint discreetly.

3 Build up the darks and add more detail where necessary. The spatter remains as a suggestion of texture.

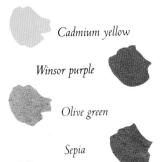

RIPENING APPLES

In the fall, the apples mature, varying in size, distribution and color. Take care when painting red apples to keep the color the same tone as the tree. Touches of warm red can "come forwards" on the picture plane and are emphasized by the complementary color of the greenery.

Controlling tone—pastel

1 *The warm light is set by the ocher-tinted paper. Start with light strokes.*

2 *Build up the foliage adding red apples in the same tone so that they do not jump forwards from the picture plane.*

3 *The apples are merely hinted at, relying on the eye to fill in the details.*

Green gray

Olive green

Sepia

Yellow ocher

Cadmium yellow

WINTER TREE

If you want an inspiring subject for winter painting you could not find a better one than the apple tree. It is compact and therefore more approachable than the larger broadleaf trees and often, because of pruning, the branches grow in angular steps in a fan-shaped structure. With a waterproof black ink line, you can enjoy the complicated surface pattern, adding a watercolor wash to complete the picture.

APPLE TREE

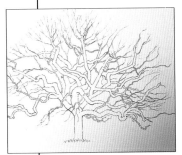

Pen and wash—ink and watercolor

1 Carefully ink in the structure of the tree with a good-quality, fibre-tip waterproof pen.

2 Wet the surface and drop in touches of Antwerp blue for the cool winter sky.

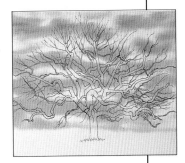

3 Once dry, add a brown wash to the tree, taking it over the sky for tonal variation. The rough paper adds bark-like texture.

Raw umber

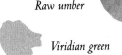

Viridian green

Antwerp blue

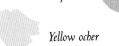

Yellow ocher

TREE DIRECTORY

This Directory includes trees from around the world chosen for their popularity and particular characteristics. Each tree is painted to demonstrate a particular technique or approach in a range of media. The Directory is divided into four parts: broad-leaf trees, conifers, palms and flower and fruit trees. If the specific tree you want to paint is not included, most of the basic shapes and textures of canopy, leaf and bark can be found here and then adapted to your needs.

BROAD-LEAF TREES

Most broad-leaf trees, such as the oak, ash or beech, are deciduous, and drop their leaves for part of the year. However, there are exceptions, such as the olive which is evergreen. Deciduous trees change with the seasons, often with flowers or catkins in the spring and decorative fruit or seeds in the fall, making them an exciting prospect for the artist.

▼ *George Gibson, In the churchyard, watercolor.*

▼ *Shadows cast by overhanging foliage are particularly obvious on a pale, smooth tree trunk. This artist has first painted the light brown trunk, with slight variations in tone to indicate curvature. Then, once the paint was dry, he added dappled shadows in a much darker version of the brown trunk mix to create the effect of warm sunlight.*

▲ *A dead branch jutting out at an irregular angle is an effective device for breaking up the canopy shape. This twisting branch creates interesting negative shapes against the featureless sky. Notice how the darker shadows on the underside of the larger branches make them look three-dimensional.*

▶ *Pale greens have been applied in an initial wash, with the stronger greens painted wet-on-dry. To accentuate the feeling of depth, sky holes have been left to show through the carefully painted branches and foliage. Both pale and dark green hues were created from the same mix of Prussian blue, indigo and cadmium yellow, but mixed with varying amounts of water.*

ASH

The common ash is one of the largest deciduous trees of Europe, growing to 100ft (30m), and similar to the white, or American ash, which is widespread throughout the mid and eastern United States. Characteristically, the tree has a long trunk which is often forked, with branches coming from it at a sharp angle, and an open canopy which is less dense than those of the oak or beech. In this watercolor painting the artist concentrates on the characteristic s-shape of the branches which often swoop down and then return up at the ends.

Burnt sienna

Yellow ocher

Sepia

Dip pen—watercolor

1 *The trunks and branches are worked between the leaves of the canopy. Vary the color and tone.*

2 *Continue building up the canopy, adding further leaves with a dip pen.*

3 *Once the tree is dry, loosely paint in the distant view and the sky with dilute paint.*

ELM

Sadly, the elm is now a rare sight on both sides of the Atlantic due to the ravages of Dutch elm disease. The English elm's characteristically massive trunk goes on up through the center of the tree with branches coming from it laterally. The canopy is dense and often hides the trunk. Build up smoky scumbles, starting with a mid-tone and adding lighter and darker layers, using the rough texture of watercolor paper to break up the brush marks. Between each application the brush is washed in water, dried on a cloth and then dipped in the prepared mix of undiluted acrylic.

Light blue violet

Sap green

Naples yellow

Scumbling— acrylic

1 *The background is laid on in thin washes of acrylic. Once dry, scumble the first layer of mid-tone green.*

2 *Once dry, work on a lighter green layer, spreading out the paint into a thin smoky film.*

3 *Scumble small touches of yellow highlights balanced by darker shadow greens.*

POPLAR

Capturing the imagination of artists wherever it grows, the poplar comes in many shapes and sizes and belongs, like the aspen, to the willow family. Possibly the best known is the tall, plume-like Lombardy poplar, often seen bordering rivers or providing a windbreak. The silver poplar has leaves with silver undersides which catch the light in a breeze. When painting wet-in-wet with watercolors, you can control the addition of wet color better if you allow previous layers to dry and then re-wet the precise area into which you want to work.

Wet-in-wet—watercolor

1 *The under-painting is laid down in a warm cadmium yellow to capture the golden evening light.*

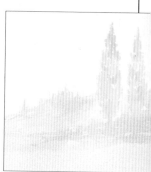

2 *Allow the paint to dry, then rewet the tree area with water before dropping in the mid-tone green.*

3 *Add further darker green shadows in the same way, but make sure you leave some yellow highlights.*

Emerald green

Burnt sienna

Chrome orange

40

SYCAMORE PLANE

The tallest broad-leaf tree in the United States, the American sycamore is a popular shade-tree, like its European counterpart, the London plane. In both species, rough-textured, dangling seed balls dot the winter tree. Both trees also have bark that looks like Nature's equivalent to superimposed watercolor washes—layers of peeling silver, gray, brown and green. Using pastels, try integrating the colors of this magical bark with overlapping feathered strokes.

Blue gray

Olive green

Sepia

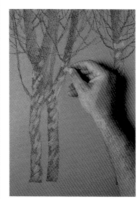

Feathering— pastel

1 *Map out the trunks with a piece of pastel held horizontally. Now use pale feathering strokes for the dappled bark.*

2 *Build up the bark with further feathering, knitting the area together with one stroke worked into the next.*

3 *Add the sky with similar feathered strokes and a sketchy background to set the scale of these tall sycamores.*

WILLOW

An ornamental tree originating in China, the weeping willow is perhaps the best known of the willow family. Arched branches give way to trailing, whip-like shoots which bear glossy, slender, rich green leaves. The weeping willow is often found on river-banks, where its lower foliage comes down to finger the passing current. To build up the layers of greens from a very pale yellow-green to darker shadows, previous layers can be preserved with strokes of a wax crayon applied under water-based paint.

**Wax resist—
watercolor**

1 *Lay on the first yellow layer, then take a clear wax crayon or sharpened candle and reserve highlight strokes.*

2 *Now build up washes over the top. The wax repels the watercolor so the yellow highlights are reserved.*

3 *Re-establish the darks in the tree and landscape to balance the contrasts.*

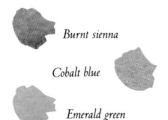

Burnt sienna

Cobalt blue

Emerald green

EUCALYPTUS GUM TREE

With their decorative bark—
the bluish blue gum, the
reddish cider gum—unusual
evergreen foliage and odor
which is supposed to keep
away mosquitoes, the
eucalyptus is understandably a
popular tree for both artist
and plantsman alike. By tinting
an underpainting with, say, red
or blue, and allowing it to
show through in places, you
can influence the temperature
of the painting as well as
holding together the various
elements of the composition.

Red underpainting —acrylic

1 *Over a red underpainting which explores tone and texture, start building up the foliage.*

2 *Continue building up the foliage from dark to light, allowing touches of red to show through.*

3 *Build up the bark, leaving pinkish highlights, and then cut in the landscape colors around the tree.*

Cerulean blue

Oxide of chromium

Naphthol crimson

HORSE CHESTNUT

The horse chestnut offers wonderful visual variety for artists. Giant, sticky buds unfurl and then candelabra-like flowers blossom in spring, followed by the "conkers" contained in prickly, green fruit beloved of schoolboys, and finally the canopy offers a glorious yellow autumn show. Sometimes a subject suggests a certain direction in your brushwork. Here the upright flowers inspired a small, vertical stroke throughout.

Ultramarine blue

Cobalt blue

Oxide of chromium

Sap green

Directional brush work— gouache

1 *Over a complementary red, add foliage greens, exploring the shadows with vertical strokes.*

2 *Now add brighter greens in the same way. Note how the tree locks in with the similarly painted sky.*

3 *Now the "candelabra" are added with a fine brush—there should not be too many, enough to inform the eye.*

OLIVE

With its silver leaves and gnarled trunk, the olive is a picturesque, evergreen tree. A common sight in orchards in the Mediterranean and California, it is tended for its summer fruit. A wonderful sight may be seen in the fall in Greece, when an olive orchard floor is carpeted with wild cyclamen. The line of the twisted trunk makes the olive a good tree to sketch. To blend colors more satisfactorily, however, try oil pastels combined with a solvent.

Blending—oil pastel and turpentine

1 *With carefully wrought parallel strokes, the twisted branches of the olives are described.*

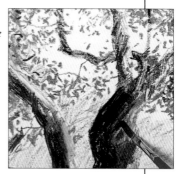

2 *To merge the colors, dip the brush in turpentine or denatured alcohol and work it into the oil pastel.*

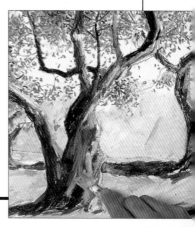

3 *Before it dries, work pale pastel into the denatured alcohol for areas of soft highlight.*

Green yellow

Phthalo green

Azure blue

Burnt umber

CONIFERS

Cypress, pine and yew are all types of conifer, which are cone-bearing trees with needles for leaves. Natives to North America and mountainous regions of the world, most conifers are evergreen, offering the artist a rich variety of shape and size as well as the differing tones and textures of their rich, dark, textured foliage. A group of distant conifers may be suggested with deep blue hues, while a closer study of the characteristic dark foliage set against bright sunlight or snow, provides the perfect subject for a tonal composition.

▼ *A wide range of tones and colors were needed to create a sense of depth. Working from dark to light, first the deep purples, then the blue, red and yellow highlights were built up with abrupt stippling strokes.*

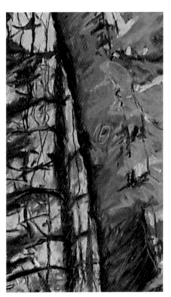

▲ *The strong verticals and horizontals of the small dead tree create an interesting tracery pattern which serves to break up the light background hues. Notice how the fine, dark lines of the branches contrast effectively with the cooler, broader trunk.*

▲ *Mary Ellen Pitts, Ribbons of sunshine, pastel.*

◀ Dark and light green hues have been applied with short, sharp strokes, giving the impression of prickly pine needles. The delicate, irregular branches add extra interest to the crucial sky holes.

CYPRESS

The classic plume-like cypress, common throughout the Mediterranean, is perhaps best loved for its role in Italian Renaissance paintings. The dense green foliage favors the opaque quality of gouache which can be built up in layers from dark to light to give the desirable depth of tone. Superimposed gouache tends to combine with the previous layer, even if this is dry. This characteristic can be used to bleed in color from beneath and create a variation in the top color.

Oxide of chromium

Olive green

Cobalt blue

Burnt umber

CONIFERS

Texture— gouache

1 *The morning light exaggerates tonal differences. Lay on a flat mid tone.*

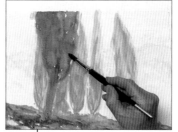

2 *Add texture with a darker tone applied in wispy lines, wet-on-dry, to describe the shape.*

3 *Add further texture to the background trees, always keeping them paler compared with the foreground tree.*

REDWOOD

Redwood trees, which have been known to exceed 300ft (100m) in height, inspire awe in all who see them, and this is reflected in their appointment as state tree of California. The velvet subtleties of their red trunks which give the family its name and the monumentality of the towering foliage, can be conveyed with bold brushwork and textural paints such as acrylics or oils. Here the artist chooses to portray the grandeur of these trees with the misty early morning light providing a horizontal foil for their strong verticality.

Highlights—oil

1 The general masses are established with thin mixes of paint diluted with equal parts of turpentine or denatured alcohol and linseed oil.

2 Highlight variations are added: first, strokes of pink-white paint are applied, then scratched into the darks with the brush end.

3 The delicate, foreground fern-like foliage is added wet-in-wet in thicker horizontal strokes in fresh greens.

Chromium green oxide

Sap green

Raw umber

FIR

Best known nowadays as the trees that cover lower alpine slopes, individual firs, or pines, create a pleasing picture of deep blue-green contrasting with the stark white of fresh snow. When using watercolor, the most effective way to highlight the virgin purity of the snow on the branches is to scrape the paint back to the white paper beneath. For this you will need a medium to heavy watercolor paper—here 140lb (300gsm).

Scratching out— watercolor

1 *Over a pale blue wash, the areas of snow are reserved with masking fluid. Now add the dark greens.*

2 *Remove the masking fluid, and then scratch in hard edges of the brightest highlight with a pointed scalpel.*

3 *Further dots of highlight are scratched out of the foreground for the sparkling snow.*

Ultramarine blue

Olive green

Sap green

Winsor violet

CEDAR

Well known in Britain as a feature of nineteenth-century country park design, this stately evergreen tree, native of the Himalayas and the Syrian Mountains, belongs to the pine family. Its rich dark tones could well be translated with oil paint in thin layers of transparent, dark blues, with lighter greens built up over the top. Pastels can be combined with other media for a particular texture. For example, you can build up a flat underpainting in watercolor or acrylics and then work the pastels over the top as in this demonstration.

Mixed media— acrylic and chalk pastel

1 *On acrylic paper, loosely plan out the base shape of the cedar, ready for the pastel work.*

2 *Once dry, work over the top with lighter pastels, redefining the form of the trunk and branches.*

3 *Take pale blue pastel over the sky area and use it to sharpen up the outline of the cedar.*

 Olive green

 Brilliant yellow green

Sap green

 Oxide of chromium

PALMS

An integral part of desert islands and coral beaches, palms come in many shapes and sizes—over 2,500 different species in all. Palms grow mostly in tropical zones but some species survive colder weather. Although evergreen, different species mark the summer with a show of wondrous fruit—dates, bananas, coconuts, berries—providing a rich variety of contrasting and complementary colors which will add interest to compositions in any medium.

▼ *Benjamin Eisenstat, Sanibel storm, watercolor.*

◄ The dramatic movement of the palm fronds bending in the wind has been captured with sweeping brush strokes painted over paler highlights. These sweeping strokes are echoed in the sky immediately behind the top branches, and above the lower branches, to enhance the impression of movement.

► The fringed foliage was painted with quick loose strokes to suggest movement, applied with a fine-pointed sable brush. A stiff mix of Prussian blue and raw sienna was used—with more blue added to the upper branches to balance the dark gray washes of racing cloud below.

DATE

The date palm grows tall and thin like the coconut palm. Other varieties such as the Canary date palm are used more for decorative purposes and are shorter with a mass of foliage. To suggest the singeing heat of a tropical day, heighten the contrasts and intensify your colors.

Up tempo color— gouache

1 *Explore the subject with an underpainting in complementary colors—yellow for blue, red for green.*

2 *Add more naturalistic colors over the top. The first layer will bleed a little into subsequent layers.*

Cadmium yellow deep

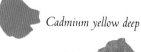
Ultramarine blue

Cadmium red pale

Sap green

Naples yellow

3 *Build up the sharp contrasts of bright light, allowing touches of white to show through for highlights.*

COCONUT

With its tall trunk and fringed leaves, and its waterside habitat, this is the artist's "typical" palm. The young leaves stand erect at the top and then bend over as they age, eventually turning brown and falling off, leaving their bases to form the next area of bark. With thicker paints, the textured effect of the dense fringed foliage and coconuts can be etched out of an area of darker paint with a scalpel so that the white support, or paler layers of paint, show through.

Cadmium yellow light

Deep violet

Ultramarine blue

Naphthol crimson

Sgraffito— acrylic

1 *Build up the tree over the sky with a coarse brush, dry-brushing the lacy fronds.*

2 *Now, with the end of a scalpel, scratch out small points of white light, taking the paint back to the white primer.*

3 *Continue scratching out these points of light to balance the deep shadows of the evening light.*

FAN

Often seen lining streets in California, the Washingtonia, similar to the European fan palm, has fan-like leaves which hang down the trunk when dead, giving it its nickname of the petticoat palm. The leaves form ellipses when seen in perspective, but the shagginess of this palm and its "petticoats" are best conceived in watercolor with a pointed brush for the linear detail over paler layers beneath.

Linear work— watercolor

1 Build up palest background washes for the distance, then superimpose the planes of the landscape.

2 Now work up washes on the tree and, with a fine-pointed sable brush held vertically, draw in the details of the foliage.

3 Add darker, fan-shaped leaves and details of the shaggy trunk to increase the three-dimensional effect.

New gamboge

Permanent rose

Raw sienna

Burnt sienna

SOLID-LEAF BANANA

The clean-cut shapes of the banana palm are ideal for the bold effect of acrylic paint applied with a knife. Although the fresh green of the unripened fruit is refreshing in itself, the vivid yellow of the more mature bananas could offer an exciting dimension of color to a painting. Start with thinner applications of paint which will sink into the paper and seal it, then add increasingly more impasto touches of acrylic with your knife.

Knife painting— acrylic

1 *Over a dark wash, sketch in the shapes of the palms with a palette knife and undiluted acrylic.*

2 *Build up the fronds with downward strokes of a No. 18 painting knife, blending colors as you go.*

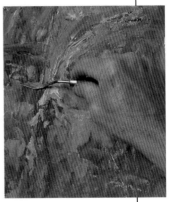

Sap green

Cadmium yellow

Dioxazine purple

3 *As the painting progresses, apply the paint in more juicy strokes, touching on the final darks with the edge of the knife.*

FLOWER AND FRUIT TREES

Trees that make a show of flowering or bearing fruit are always a joy to paint. Try capturing the waxy flowers and twisting branches of the magnolia, or the intricately shaped leaves and quirky fruit of the fig tree. Some trees automatically suggest a medium to be painted in because of the texture of the blossom or the reflective nature of the leaves. Try using a range of different media for an original approach.

▼ *Rosalie Stambler Nadeau, Ruggles Farm House, pastel.*

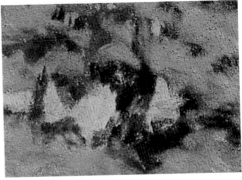

▼ Starting with the dark bluish-green, then building up to lighter hues, the artist has explored the complex shadows and highlights with lively, abrupt strokes. Only a few small dabs of complementary red and purple are needed to suggest vibrant flowers.

▲ The central sky hole is an important feature, breaking up the mid-tones of the foliage and allowing contrasting branches to show through. Rough random strokes of pale green and yellow, mixed on the canvas, plus darker touches of dark green shadow, indicate lush summer leaves.

◄ Cool shadows and warm sunlight have been expressed in a variety of tone and color. Notice how the blue foreground shadow requires a cooler mix where it covers the pale road, and a warmer tinge for the softer texture of the grass. The smooth strokes of gray paint capture the flat texture of the stone steps, and contrast effectively with the thick dabs of dark shadow and delicate points of magenta which were applied with a smaller brush.

59

ORANGE

The citrus shine of waxy oranges is ideally represented by the glossy effect of glazed oils. The simple leaf shapes should not be ignored and their intense evergreen color is brought out by the added sheen of the glaze. When mixing the colors, take care that they do not become dull or you will not be able to achieve the tart shades that are desirable.

Glazing—oils

1 *Slowly build up layers, wet-on-dry, keeping the paint thin and transparent but making it darker as you go.*

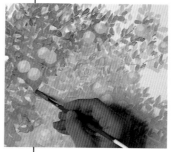

2 *Pale leaves at the edge of the canopy catch the light; in the center are darker more generalized leaves.*

3 *Add the sky, carefully cutting in around the leaves. Vary the shadowing on the oranges.*

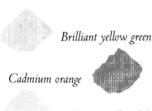

Brilliant yellow green

Cadmium orange

Cadmium yellow light

Sap green

MAGNOLIA

The stunning bloom of magnolia trees, characteristically occurring before the emergence of foliage, creates an attractive image of silhouetted branches embellished by crowns of elegant petals. The relief of acrylic impasto is suitable for accentuating this unusual feature, showing the clearly defined lines of the bark and the waxy opacity of the flowers. The thickness of the paint allows it to be built up without sacrificing freshness of color, enhancing the effect of light on dark.

Impasto—oils

1 Rhythm is what the magnolia tree is about. Search for it in the under-painting, establishing the main shapes.

2 Build up the background tree and then the foreground bough. Here apply thick, juicy strokes for these perfect blooms.

3 The impasto paint on the foreground flowers reflects the light, drawing the eye and adding to tonal subtleties.

Ultramarine blue

Oxide of chromium

Alizarin crimson

FIG

Although a tree of tropical and subtropical climes, the fig is now commonly seen in colder countries, often growing up against a wall. A small spreading tree, the leaves are lobed, thick and leathery, making a fascinating abstract pattern of shapes and cast shadows even from quite a distance. The urn-shaped fruit start off green and mature through red and purple to a deep violet. Try to use the brush shape to put across the pattern of color and tone, keeping the colors fresh.

Yellow ocher

Olive green

Cobalt blue

Burnt umber

Varying greens— watercolor

1 *To represent light on the canopy, build up colors ranging from yellow ocher to cobalt blue.*

2 *Continue to extend the canopy, painting leaves from every angle. Draw out the trunk with the painting "spoon" (see page 16).*

3 *If you are using good quality paper, for a softer image, you can wash the whole painting under cold running water.*

62

CHERRY

This much-loved tree in many shapes performs all year with stunning white or pink blossom, red-green shoots and bright green leaves in spring and early summer, red, yellow or black cherries in late summer, and scarlet, autumn foliage. When painting a cherry tree, the artist has to convey form, texture and color with minimal strokes, and this often involves a combination of techniques. The colors which make up the canopy are not only those of leaves or, in this case, blossom, but touches of the sky and background trees glimpsed beyond.

Alizarin crimson

Prussian blue

Cadmium yellow

Stippling— watercolor

1 *Lay in washes of pale pink for the cherry blossom. Start adding stippled greens for the background trees.*

2 *Fill in the sky and then stipple the blue in amongst the pink blossom.*

3 *For more depth, further stipple brighter pink onto the blossom with a small brush.*

CREDITS

Quarto would like to thank all the artists who have kindly allowed us to reproduce their work in this book.

We would also like to thank the following artists for their help in the demonstrations of techniques: Jean Canter, David Carr, Patrick Cullen, Margaret Glass, Ted Gould, Paul Kenny, Kay Ohsten, Alan Oliver, Ian Sidaway.

Senior art editor Clare Baggaley
Designer Rachael Stone
Design assistant Steve Tse
Editor Cathy Marriott
Copy editor Diana Craig
Photographer Colin Bowling
Illustrator Neil Ballpit
Picture researcher Miriam Hyman
Picture research manager Giulia Hetherington
Art director Moira Clinch
Assistant art director Penny Cobb
Editorial director Mark Dartford

Photographic credits

Key: a above, b below, c centre, l left, r right
Moira Clinch 5l, 7b
Giulia Hetherington 6r
John Hyman 4b, 5c, 6l, 7a
Windrush Photos 5bcr, br, 11

Typeset by Central Southern Typesetters, Eastbourne
Manufactured by Bright Arts Pte Ltd, Singapore
Printed by Leefung-Asco Printers Ltd, China